André Gide

by VINIO ROSSI

Columbia University Press

NEW YORK & LONDON 1968

COLUMBIA ESSAYS ON MODERN WRITERS is a series of critical studies of English, Continental, and other writers whose works are of contemporary artistic and intellectual significance.

Editor: William York Tindall

Advisory Editors
Jacques Barzun   W. T. H. Jackson   Joseph A. Mazzeo   Justin O'Brien

André Gide is Number 35 of the series

VINIO ROSSI is Associate Professor of French at Oberlin College. He is the author of *André Gide: The Evolution of an Aesthetic.*

Passages from the works of André Gide are quoted, in the author's own translation, through the kind permission of Editions Gallimard, Secker & Warburg, Ltd., and Alfred A. Knopf. *Journal* refers to the Pléiade edition of Gide's journals and memoirs.

André Gide

Throughout all his life and work André Gide (1869–1951) searched for plenitude, a plenitude which would balance and satisfy the needs engendered by various aspects of his personality: a persistent inclination toward mysticism and introspection; an ever-present temptation to indulge in pleasures of the flesh; a need for rational testing and recording of experience. It took Gide the better part of eighty years to achieve some degree of fullness of experience and to reconcile antinomies within himself. He had progeny, he made peace with his God, he experienced the intensities of human existence, and he left behind him his complete works. "For the good of future humanity, I have done my work. I have lived" (*Thésée*).

If in eighty-two years Gide managed to accomplish so much, it took him at least the first twenty-four to formulate and to see the virtues of plenitude. Formed by the rigorous Protestant ethic of his widowed mother and her companion, Anna Shackleton, Gide spent his early life attempting to enforce an ethic of exclusion; he denied the sensual, the temporal, the real in favor of the spiritual, the eternal, and the imaginary world. He was ideally suited for the Symbolist movement, or so it seemed from his first book, *Les Cahiers d'André Walter* (1891). But nothing human can be suppressed successfully, Gide was to learn through experience. The more his hero tried to follow the ascetic path, the more he felt tempted by the scenic route; moreover, temptations overcome made him vulnerable to the sins of pride. Distraught by his own ambivalent nature, by the evanescent world of his mind, by the ambiguity of his relationship with his cousin and intended wife, and, finally, by all his sensual contact with the world, André Walter dies of brain fever and of the hallucinations he learned to invoke with ease.

The first important result achieved by the publication of *Les Cahiers* was to bring Gide into contact with the reality of Parisian literary circles. He met Maurice Barrès and Oscar Wilde, was introduced to most of the prominent symbolists, frequented Mallarmé's Tuesday evenings and Hérédia's Saturday afternoons. He decided to make a place for himself in the literary whirl. A first choice was identifying himself as a symbolist. The second was to justify this choice by composing a theory of the symbol, *Le Traité du Narcisse* (1891), and a symbolic travelogue, *Le Voyage d'Urien* (1893). Although not the account of a real voyage, as the pun in the title suggests ("le voyage du rien"), the book represents nevertheless a timid step in the direction of a broader experience of life; Gide's imaginary travelers make their way through three landscapes representing as many responses to life: the sensual ("Sur une mer pathétique"), the introspective ("La mer des Sargasses"), and the ascetic ("La mer glaciale"). The last still best suits his nature, and the second still tempts him, but he has grown enough to consider, however indirectly and negatively, the first and most troubling of his own interior landscapes.

But he evidently did not succeed in convincing himself of the evils of the flesh: he returned to the theme in his next work, *La Tentative amoureuse* (1893). Gide argues here that passion is self-consuming and hence destructive, that desire satisfied produces boredom, self-satisfaction, and complacency, that the pleasures of the flesh can addict and dissolve the will. He presents the case in the form of a journey through the seasons of the year and in the person of two young lovers, Luc and Rachel. Even before a year passes, both Luc and Gide become impatient with this love affair. Luc abandons Rachel in the hope of finding "new things"; Gide, abandoning both hurriedly, ends the story with similar aspirations.

Gide finished *La Tentative amoureuse* during the summer of 1893, at about the time he and his friend, Paul-Albert Laurens, decided to travel south to North Africa to spend the year broadening their experience and fulfilling themselves. So radical a decision to explore the real world was prepared well in advance. For some time Gide had been gathering sufficient energy and arguments to break away from family, country, God, and his own pious impulses. During June, 1891, he found in Laforgue's writings a kindred spirit that encouraged him to develop a measure of objectivity flavored with irony; conversations with Oscar Wilde provoked a certain boldness in his thought and in the realization of his uniqueness; a visit to Munich in March and April, 1892, affirmed his growing independence from his mother, as did the discovery of Goethe's plays which he had both read and seen there; and another experiment in independent traveling, in Spain during August, 1893, further drew the young introspective out of himself and into the world of sensation. Finally, credit for Gide's gradual emergence into the real world is also due to the simple and sensual poetry of Francis Jammes and the pleasant summer months spent in the company and on the grounds of the Laurens family.

The *Journal* entries of 1893 document Gide's transformation. On March 17, while visiting relatives at Montpellier, just before leaving for Spain, Gide notes, "I love life and prefer sleep not because of its nothingness but because of dreams." The following entries of a month or so later reveal a change in attitude that was fully realized finally by the decision in October to leave for North Africa.

I know that when I want to partake of those things which I had denied myself because of their beauty it will not be like a sinner,

[5]

in secret, with the bitterness of repentance; no, it will be without remorse, with force and joy. Leave the dream world at last and live a full and forceful life.

No longer read books by ascetics. Find exaltation elsewhere; admire the difficult joy of equilibrium, the joy of life's plenitude. May each thing offer all possible life it contains. It is a duty to make oneself happy.

Throughout the *Journal* from April to October, 1893, Gide rejects ever more boldly his former ethic of exclusion and his pious yearnings for fulfillment in the kingdom of Absolutes. He speaks of becoming robust, happy, normal, of abandoning himself to life, of putting the various aspects of his personality in equilibrium and in harmony. He even goes further, seeing happiness and the highest form of originality in the absence of limits and scruples, in accepting, even seeking, all sorts of experience that the human organism can possibly undergo. The following year, after his trip to North Africa, Gide formulated this principle: "I am done with any system of morality that does not allow or teach the most noble, the most beautiful, and the most liberal use and development of our forces." Repeating later on in the 1894 *Journal* entries other statements of this sort, he underscores the consciousness and deliberateness of his search for plenitude.

In North Africa Gide got more than he had bargained for and almost more than he could handle: an attack of tuberculosis and the subsequent slow convalescence in the desert town of Biskra intensified his physical reawakening and immersion in the real world of sensations. Yet, the first book Gide wrote and published after *La Tentative amoureuse* and the first North African sojourn was not an ode to joy, but rather a mad piece of folly, the first sustained example of Gide's humor. *Paludes* (1894) originated in early 1893 but was not composed until the fall of the following year while Gide was continuing his cure in the cool mountain air of Neuchâtel. Because his reawakening was so recent, and because he was anticipating returning to Biskra for the oncoming winter, it is not surprising that the "new" Gide should look back at his past nor that he should, fortified with a newly won objectivity, treat this past with avenging irony. But what is even more interesting is that this first expression of the new Gide contains a sense of the comic that announces in many ways his subsequent work.

Gide himself has characterized his sense of humor as anchored in an inclination toward the bizarre, the illogical, and the unexpected. It expresses, some say, the mind's refusal to take seriously a suffocating world. Others have suggested that Gide's humor serves to mask problems that preoccupy him, enabling him to experiment with possible solutions casually and without the inhibiting effects of stage fright. From 1893 to 1895, when he was struggling both to free himself from his mother's influence and to define for himself the role and nature of the artist, he repeated on several occasions that everything in the truly original artist must appear new, that he alone has the key to a special world of his own.

He must have a particular philosophy, aesthetics, ethics; his entire work tends only to result in revealing these. And that is what makes his style. I have also discovered, and this is very important, that he has to have a particular way of joking, a particular sense of humor. (*Journal*, I, 94.)

Not all that is funny in Gide's writing and reported conversations can be classified under one type of humor or be made to fit within the category of his special sense of humor. In the journals, in much of the autobiographical material, and in some of the imaginative works, Gide's jokes range through most of the familiar categories, from low lusty humor to high-brow word and sound plays. Even within the framework of the *soties*, as he came to call his comic works, there is a variety of humor. Nevertheless, a point of view establishes a context of

[7]

humor in the *soties* that is both peculiarly Gidian and rigorously consistent with the totality of Gide's world. On several occasions Gide uses the adjective *saugrenu* to describe his sense of humor. It means bizarre, absurd, ridiculous, and tends to describe, in Gide's use, the vigorous but incongruent confrontation of two systems of thought or associations, that is, the confrontation of two or more words, ideas, events, each of which suggests a frame of reference only apparently related to the others. At the basis of Gide's whimsy there is an eruption of illogic within a context promising logic or, at worst, treated as logically coherent. Because, then, the *saugrenu* operates on two levels, the level of incongruency and the suggested level of congruency, it is closely related to irony; it suggests what might be while falling short of the potential, remaining schematic, incomplete, or stunted.

There are many examples of this type of humor outside of the *soties*, in the *Journal*, in the memoirs, but none so succinct perhaps as two notations from *Paludes*.

Lane bordered with birthwort.

"Why, dear friend," said I, "with a still uncertain sky, have you brought only one umbrella?"
"It's a parasol," she answered.

In the first example a lyrical description clashes with a cacophonous learned term and reveals a rather misguided eagerness for precision. In the second, a basically insignificant question is elevated to a level of serious and earnest inquiry by a vague preciosity of language; it is thereupon met with the same cuteness of formulation which has a logic all its own, yet does not relate to the reality of the situation except on a purely linguistic level. Angèle, the narrator's interlocutor and companion, is perfectly rigorous in her logic of compromise: in the face of uncertain weather, rather than being caught with no umbrella at all or left carrying two to no avail, she compromises. Her choice is as logical as drizzle. But further rendering the exchange entirely nonsensical, the two major nouns ("ombrelle" and "en-tout-cas") mean essentially the same thing: "parasol."

In his memoirs, *Si le grain ne meurt*, Gide attributes the tone of these notations and his ability to sustain it to a mood he can describe only by the English word "estrangement." Because of his illness and long-anticipated sensual reawakening in North Africa, because of his eagerness to return after his Swiss convalescence, Gide naturally felt dissociated from his erstwhile self and comrades. He was striving to live in contingency, to absorb it and delight in it, while they persisted in rejecting it. But his feelings of estrangement were all too familiar to him and were an integral part of his personality. He confesses to a sort of dissociation from reality and to a disbelief in the reality of the world on numerous occasions throughout his life. Mentioned early in the *Journal* and frequently thereafter in various forms, recalled in *Si le grain ne meurt* in several contexts, his difficulty again crops up at the very end of his life in *Ainsi soit-il* in this succinct form: "I have never been able to *adhere* perfectly to reality." Such a handicap, better described as an inability to possess himself fully, to integrate a sense of self with emotion, thought, and sensation, explains the structure of his world view, his lifelong search for and idealization of plenitude and equilibrium as well as, eventually, his sense of humor. "What exalts us is the feeling of plenitude," Gide remarked in his journal shortly before his first voyage to North Africa. And in the same important entry he articulated the opposite notion: "What makes us laugh is the feeling of atrophy in something capable of fullness. All things," he concludes, "have within them the potential for plenitude."

It seems reasonable, on the basis of these and similar remarks made at so important a period in his life, to use them as guides for a discussion of his fiction. In addition to revealing the personal aspirations articulated early in life and maintained to its very end, these remarks suggest aesthetic analogues which, together with the problem of point of view, lie at the core of Gide's fictional technique. The evolution of atrophy in a personality fully capable of attaining fullness, traced from either a subjective or an objective point of view, yielded works of art Gide felt obliged to distinguish as either *récits* or *soties*. Viewed objectively, the results are comic; told from the vantage point of the victim, they are tragic. But in either case they are personality deformations that keep their victims from realizing a full measure of their potential.

The main fault of his protagonist in *Paludes*, which in the preface Gide called a sickness, is precisely his inability to ignore the stifling swamplike world he lives in. He sees nothing but mediocrity all about him, in his friends and in himself as well. But he is trapped in circumstances basically of his own making; victim of an obsession which transforms his vision of the world, which in turn increases his feelings of "boredom, monotony, futility," he finds himself caught in an ever-narrowing spiral that brings the isolated fault of his personality to its conclusion in absurdity. The protagonist, potentially a full, round character, is flat, deformed, and atrophied by his obsession.

Gide's *Paludes* is composed of the daily journal entries of a man of letters and excerpts from the book, *Paludes*, that he is busy writing. In the central episode, a mock symposium sponsored by his friend, Angèle, he demonstrates his talent for transforming a variety of stimuli into terms consistent with his obsession. He describes his book in ways most appropriate to his interlocutors: for the physiologist, *Paludes* is the story of animals whose eyes have atrophied as a result of living in the dark caves; for the critic, he quotes Vergil, and borrows Tityrus as his own hero; for the psychologist, the book is the story of the normal man, the proto-personality everyone takes as the point of departure for his own development; for the moralist, it is a didactic work whose motive is to spur people to action; and, for the group as a whole, "Paludes, at this moment," he says, "is the story of Angèle's reception." But the process is not unconscious; he explains that the only way to tell a story so that everyone will understand it is to change its form in line with each new psychological and intellectual orientation. And, in fact, when he describes *Paludes* to his very active friend, Hubert, he recounts Tityre's adventures—or non-adventures—day by day to the point of boring him. For the calm and delicate Angèle, his account verges at times on the tabloid human interest story with interspersed discussions of fictional techniques.

Given the narrator's obsession, together with his lucidity and his desire to change, how does he break out of his distasteful situation? He cannot, of course, and every attempt to move, to change his ways is frustrated, primarily by his own timidity and inertia. Nothing comes of his visits to the hothouses of the Jardin des Plantes, except imagery for his book; his voyage to a suburban park aborts as well; he does not even finish his book but begins another with a similar paludal title, *Polders*. It is not surprising then to discover, alongside the swamp image and the attendant ideas of immobility, images that suggest enclosure and confinement. Nouns like "doors," "gates," "windows," "curtains," "courtyards," adjectives of limitations, like "small," "closed," "narrow," "circular," and so on abound in the narrator's journal. The more obsessed he becomes, the more desperately he idealizes the contrary: the new, the unexpected, departures, voyages, action, freedom, and, especially, spontaneity.

Stagnancy horrifies him. At Angèle's banquet, he informs the hostess that nothing irritates him more than "what goes round and round in place." Like the fan in her apartment, he and his friends are not truly immobile yet they do no more than move about in place. They, too, are stagnant. Their acts have become habits and thus the receptacle of their personality; they define themselves not by the style of an action, but by the action itself. But it is not only their own innate "normality" that encourages them along the easy path; everything urges them to lapse into a rut: "and that's just what irritates me: everything outside, laws, customs, even the sidewalks seem to determine our relapses and ensure our monotony." That the narrator himself cannot avoid such relapses is a point hammered home by the failure of his paltry little trip. He himself incarnates the very stagnancy he cannot abide and, further, develops it to its extreme. In effect, Gide's narrator enacts in his own way the principle suggested in one of the "remarkable sentences" listed at the end of the *sotie*, "one must carry out to their conclusion all the ideas one has raised."

The major characters of *Le Prométhée mal enchaîné* (1899) also bring to some sort of conclusion the ideas they raise and, as a consequence, at least two of them emerge deformed. Gide's second *sotie* is made up of events which are as bizarre as the moods and futile gestures of his first. One May afternoon on the boulevards of Paris the "Miglionnaire" banker, Zeus, delivers unsolicited and randomly a 500-franc bank note to an undistinguished human being and, also at random, rewards another's kindness with a vigorous slap in the face. Meanwhile, Prometheus, tired of his long sojourn in the Caucasian mountains, sheds his shackles and goes for a walk in Paris. At a café he meets Damocles and Cocles, the recipients of Zeus' largesse, who recount their stories and describe the transformations their lives have undergone since they were singled out. Damocles is obsessed by the sudden and inexplicable receipt of the bank note while Cocles wins sympathy for his misfortune. As his misfortunes grow (he loses an eye), he continues to seek them out knowing he will profit from the sympathy of others (he receives the directorship of a large foundation to aid the blind). Damocles, on the other hand, cannot explain why he received the money and is tortured by the impossibility of finding its source and of repaying, or at least thanking, the unknown donor.

Because of Zeus' gesture, both have risen from the anonymous mass of people and have gained an identity. Because Damocles received money and can neither explain nor repay it, he discovers he has scruples; Cocles, unjustly victimized, becomes the underdog that seeks and attracts sympathy. Each nourishes and imbues his new identity with his whole being. The man with the eagle recognizes himself in both the man with one eye and the man with the cross of debt. Prometheus, pondering these developments, concludes that everyone must possess an identity to which he can devote himself: we must all have an eagle of our own which we can feed with our very substance.

But, as Prometheus nourishes his eagle, he diminishes as it flourishes. Similarly, Damocles, so distraught by the dilemma that defines him, finally expends himself on it and dies of brain fever. Pondering these new developments, Prometheus reconsiders the substance of his first sermon and, for Damocles' funeral oration, comes up with a parable which he hopes will clarify the tie between Damocles' death and his own decision to kill his eagle.

The parable has as its principal characters Angèle, Tityrus, and two more Vergilian figures, Meliboeus and Menalcas. Tityrus, surrounded by swamps and inertia, is prodded into activity by Menalcas "who planted an idea in Tityrus' head and a seed in the swamp before him." The seed grows first into a plant and then into a gigantic oak to which Tityrus devotes himself and around which develops a settlement he eventually administers. Angèle, the librarian, invites the reluctant Tityrus to take a trip to Paris where Meliboeus, the naked, Pan-like, flute-playing free spirit, takes Angèle with him to Rome. Tityrus, thus abandoned, finds himself once again at home, alone, and surrounded by swamps. The audience titters a bit, charmed by the humor in Tityrus' simplicity and circular busyness. But they do not fully grasp Prometheus' apparent reversal of position; the appearance itself of a sense of humor in one who had earlier claimed "an irremediably serious turn of mind" so disconcerts them that they laugh also from nervousness. Happy that he has been able to please them, Prometheus admits that he has found, since Damocles' death, the secret of laughter. One cannot help trying to clarify this secret by resorting to Gide's own ideas on similar matters: laughter arises from atrophy and from the objectivity that permits the perception of a stunted growth as caricature.

Prometheus is astounded to discover that Zeus refuses to keep eagles, he just distributes them. This revelation contradicts his basic principle and undermines his commitment to his own eagle. More damage is done to his original principle when he sees in Damocles the effect of excess devotion to one's eagle. Through Damocles' death, Prometheus realizes that death is the limit beyond which one cannot develop an idea in oneself, that developing an idea to such an extreme is costly and prevents knowing other ideas. Prometheus realizes, in short, that unless he is careful, his eagle will end by devouring him completely. Such objectivity affords Prometheus a gauge to measure the excess of his beliefs and the degree of their complicity in Damocles' death. He now realizes that he need not forfeit all control to his eagle, that, though committed to an idea, he need not relinquish his autonomy, his freedom. Before leaving the Caucasus, he had rid himself of "chains, tenons, straitjackets, parapets, and other scruples" which were "ankylosing him," and "between four and five in autumn, he strolled down the boulevard which goes from the Madeleine to the Opéra"; similarly in his fable, Tityrus, feeling that his "occupations, responsibilities, and various scruples held him no more than the great oak," smiled and left, "taking with him the money box and Angèle, and toward evening strolled with her down the boulevard which goes from the Madeleine to the Opéra."

Tityrus, too, discovers laughter when he discovers his freedom. It is basically neither futile nor tragic that the exercise of his new freedom ultimately leads him nowhere, that he has not progressed, that he returns to the neutral terrain he began on. Though abandoning himself to events, and ideas, and seeds, he does not abdicate his will power and his control, so that when he needs them he can overcome his eagles and retain the potential to grow. The new Tityrus does not stagnate. "An idea," Gide says in the *Journal*, "continues to be a living force so long as all the nourishment in it is not used up in phenomena." Once it has been used up, it promotes stagnancy and destruction unless it is abandoned. "Was it of no use, then?" they ask Prometheus after having eaten the eagle. "Don't say that, Cocles! Its flesh has nourished us. When I questioned it, it answered nothing. But I have eaten it without rancor: had it made me suffer less, it would have been less fat; less fat it would have been less delectable." Prometheus does not entirely reverse his previous position. Everyone must devote himself to his eagle, every idea must be brought to its furthest limit. But there are times when one must go beyond it, abandon it, or bring it to complete fruition outside of the self; otherwise one endangers one's health and full development. Prometheus survives the story in good health and spirits, feasts upon the eagle, and writes this book with one of its quills.

The work of art, precisely, allows the exceptional man to

accomplish what he feels capable of without adverse consequences; it permits him a plenitude and an equilibrium which are, as Gide noted in 1897, "realizable only in the work of art." The mechanics of this procedure were outlined years later by Gide in an often quoted letter: "How many buds we carry in ourselves, dear Scheffer, which bloom only in a book. . . . my recipe for creating a hero is quite simple: take one of these buds, put it in a pot—all alone—soon one has an admirable individual." Gide evidently permitted three unlikely characters to grow in his *sotie* along lines dictated by different approaches to a basic tenet of his early ethical code which he imagistically synthesized in Prometheus' devotion to his eagle: in *Les Cahiers d'André Walter* and in *Le Traité du Narcisse*, Gide formulated this tenet by saying "we must all manifest, we must all represent"; he later developed it in a pamphlet, "Quelques réflexions sur la littérature et la morale," published first in 1897 and again in 1899 as an appendix to *Le Prométhée mal enchaîné*.

In *Les Caves du Vatican* (1914) the preoccupations of the earlier *soties*, concerning action, freedom, personal identity, are brought into society. Despite the hubbub and social confusion of *Paludes*, the prime concern is the point of view of the narrator and diarist. In *Le Prométhée*, too, Gide emphasizes the relationship of his caricatures to themselves. In *Les Caves*, he is again concerned with man's relationship to himself and with the nature and function of identity, but here these preoccupations are placed in a social context; people interact with one another and their actions have social consequences. This slight change in point of view is reflected in the very form of the novel. Like a blown-up philosophical tale in the manner of Voltaire, *Les Caves* is handled with the traditional narrative tools Gide had previously avoided: the third-person narrative with frequent plunges into the interior world of its characters; intrusion of the author's comments and opinions on the matter at hand; detailed, descriptive passages of place and person; deliberate excursions into exposition of background and history of events and people; and, more subtly, a multiplicity of tones which coincide with the subject matter. *Les Caves* is essentially a traditional novel of adventure simplified and pushed to the extreme of parody.

The novel is divided into five parts, each bearing as title the name of one of the major figures. Like Damocles and Cocles, each of the figures is so devoted to his eagle that he has atrophied and become one with it: Anthime Armand-Dubois, behaviorist and mechanistic scientist, a pillar of the society of Freemasons and a militant atheist; Julius de Baraglioul, traditionalist in politics, religion, and aesthetics, a novelist convinced of the immutability of the novel of psychological analysis, of the consistency of human behavior, and of the inscrutability of the French Academy; Amédée Fleurissoire, a sincere and devoted believer, manufacturer of religious articles, a latter-day poor man's Parsifal or Sir Galahad. Even Protos (protagonist of the chapter entitled "les Mille-Pattes," the name of the international organization of outlaws he leads), who is ever present and constantly changing form and disguises, who advocates freedom and flexibility, is fixed by his need and program to oppose the staid members of the society he lives in. Only Lafcadio is free enough both socially and emotionally to be lawless and flexible like Prometheus. Though he too is a caricature, he becomes so enviable and attractive that Gide almost filled out his portrait with flesh and bone; at the end of *Les Caves* he is very nearly a round character, moving about in a two-dimensional world.

The people of *Les Caves* are divided into two groups, the select minority Protos calls "the subtle ones" and, by far the greater, "the crustaceans." To the first group belong only Protos and Lafcadio. But the qualities that make Lafcadio a

[17]

"subtle one" serve no goal other than his own enrichment, whereas in Protos, who is as subtle and cunning as the Devil himself, they are subservient to his need to dominate and oppose. Lafcadio was formed, without the rigors of family, by his courtesan mother and the talents of her successive lovers. Completely free and spontaneous, a creature of inconsistency, victim only of an insatiable curiosity that prompts him to act, Lafcadio lives heedless of consequences in a manner idealized by his complete opposite, the narrator of *Paludes*. Capable of any action that tests and reveals him, Lafcadio feels his grip is "large enough to embrace all of humanity, or perhaps to strangle it." So far he has not committed a harmful act, but realizing that the difference between harmful and beneficial is slight for the man of action at the moment of action, he becomes interested in all the unforeseen elements in an act of violence. As a result he hurls Amédée Fleurissoire from the train compartment they are sharing between Rome and Naples.

The consequences of this act go beyond the exaltation surrounding the event and reach into the calm lucid moments. "I lived oblivious," he tells young Geneviève de Baraglioul; "I killed as though in a dream, a nightmare in which I've been floundering ever since." Oblivious because he was unaware, as Protos informs him later, that one cannot live lawlessly, that even the "millipedes" have a rigid code and discipline, that one cannot "move out of one society so simply, without immediately falling into another; or that any society can do without laws." Circumstances are so manipulated by Gide that the decision to accept responsibility for Fleurissoire's death depends on Lafcadio alone. At first he threatens to do so; by the end of the book, however, the narrator suggests that he will not give himself up so easily. Lafcadio can, like Prometheus, rise above a situation and continue to exercise his freedom.

This is not so for the crustaceans of the book, nearly all of whom change one eagle for another, one fixed identity for another, one society with its system of laws for another just as stringently legalized. Miraculously cured of rheumatism, Anthime becomes a Catholic only to return to his old ways after Fleurissoire's death; Julius changes aesthetics and psychology based upon the example of gratuitous and inconsistent behavior offered by Lafcadio but reverts when he is elected to the Academy. Even in Fleurissoire a waning pious fervor promises radical changes whose full development is cut short by Lafcadio's act.

In *Les Caves* Gide dramatizes the consequences of gratuitous acts as well as those obtaining from a change in identity. In the latter case he appears to test Prometheus' final hypothesis, concluding that, once atrophied by devotion to an idea, one is so deformed that atrophy remains even if the idea passes. Atrophy, as Gide means it, is the wasting away of a whole organism that results from improper nourishment or exercise of some of its important elements. He exemplifies atrophy by fragmenting the human personality, exaggerating a few distinctive traits and virtually excluding the rest. Now, depending upon the manner and the context in which these dominant traits are presented artistically, they become either exaggerations in caricature or tragic flaws. A constant danger for Gide was too close identification with his characters. Understandably alarmed, he noted in his 1912 journal that his puppets in *Les Caves* were getting out of hand and rounding out with blood and bones; "they are forcing me to take them more and more seriously." Maintaining his characters at the level of caricature was essential to a free working out of ideas he considered important. The obvious consequence of getting closer to his characters and treating them sympathetically would have been to undermine the whimsy of the *sotie* and inhibit his freedom. But even more dangerous, this seriousness would have transformed his work from caricature to tragedy. A key device, though not used in the first of the *soties*, is the objective third-person narrative, which gave Gide a distance from his characters that freed his whimsy and enabled him to see and depict the ridiculousness in certain modes of seriousness and ultra-serious behavior. Conversely, the first-person narrative presents a case subjectively and without the perspective that establishes some reasonable hierarchy of values. Unless this device is handled ironically, as Gide did in *Paludes*, it lessens the distance between author or reader and the characters, evokes sympathy, and sets the scene for tragedy.

Jean Hytier noted that the *soties* are stories in which wisdom bears the mask of folly while the *récits* reveal the folly under the appearance of wisdom (Hytier, *André Gide*, p. 67). Essentially, then, the *récit* is the reverse side of the *sotie*, distinguished by means of aesthetic devices alone. But the stuff each is made of is the same: atrophy of the human personality presented either from the point of view of the victim or from some objective point of view.

All the *récits*, from *L'Immoraliste* (1902) to *Geneviève* (1936), tales recounted in the first person, are what Gide called critical or ironical books. *L'Immoraliste* is a book of warning, a critique of a certain form of individualism, characterized by a tendency to relinquish self-control to instincts. After the premature death of his wife, for which his own selfishness and negligence were largely responsible, Michel finds himself alone, independent, and free. But after three months of abandon, he realizes that "knowing how to liberate oneself is nothing; what is difficult is knowing how to be free." He summons to his side several faithful friends who sit and listen to him recount his life.

Brought up under the subtle limitations inculcated by his

Huguenot mother, he transferred this severity and ascetism, upon her death, to the rigorous task of fashioning himself after his father: at twenty he was so skilled in philology and archaeology that his father farmed out research projects to him. Later, to satisfy his father's deathbed wish, he agrees to marry without quite knowing, at twenty-four, what marriage or life can entail. The first part of the book traces Michel's evolution from a concern with dead things to the discovery and taste for life, from a vague awareness of his own sentiments to a need for sensation, from a context of abstraction to a world of concrete things. Although he begins truly to see the world with the help of his wife, it is the severe attack of tuberculosis and subsequent slow convalescence in North Africa that reawakens him to life and to himself. In his search for health he establishes a simple and simplistic ethic that is finally carried beyond his convalescence: everything healthful and healthy is good while all else is evil. Because his early education, and all the conventions of society it perpetuates, offer resistance to his self-revelation, he brands them as evil and evolves an antisocial, antiestablishment doctrine that rejects artifice, culture, restraint, and intellect. He relinquishes his will and abandons himself to his instincts, in the hope of casting off the new man and reaching the authentic, or "old," man the Bible speaks of.

Like Anthime Armand-Dubois, Michel falls into a system as rigid as the one he would escape. But he does not succeed in changing himself as thoroughly as he thinks he does. He carries over many intellectual needs that undermine the fulfillment of his hedonistic doctrine: his needs for strategy, for rational justification, and, mostly, for some authority against whom to react. Marceline takes on this last role; she is his last tie to civilization and as such he has to destroy her. Ménalque, on the other hand, represents the ideal Michel has set for himself: the lucid, independent, and complete utilization of one's energies. Incapable of realizing such an ethic, Michel simply abandons himself to sensation, attempting to justify and modify his behavior in reaction to the opposing ideals Ménalque and Marceline represent. Both realize, however, that Michel is eluding their influence. Marceline can do nothing to control her husband's growing selfishness. Ménalque, after noting the inconsistency in Michel's supposed disdain for property and his many possessions, finally urges Michel to keep his "calm happiness of the hearth." The last remark that Ménalque makes about Michel seems to sum up his evaluation of his would-be disciple: "One believes one possesses and, in fact, one is possessed."

Possessed indeed, to the point of dissolution of his will power, Michel cannot abandon Marceline and live the life he dreams of all alone; he drags her back with him to North Africa where she finally dies. Thereafter, unable to help himself, he needs others to tear him away from the small Algerian village he has settled in, to give him reasons for living, and to help him "prove to himself that he has not exceeded his rights."

If Michel's eagle is an obsession with sensations to the detriment of intellect and will power, Alissa's, in *La Porte étroite* (1909), is made of other stuff. Where Michel dissolves will power and exalts instinct, she denies instinct and tenses her will through continual self-abnegation. She chooses the narrow path of piety leading to God and ultimate self-denial in death. But the more she effaces herself, the more she has to prove her worth by further sacrifices. God, of course, does not respond and Alissa, in a moment of desperate solitude, cries out, "I should like to die now, quickly, before I understand once again that I am alone." Like Michel, Alissa is condemned to bring to conclusion one human tendency. As a consequence of her ascetic piety, she negates not only herself but also Jerome with whom she could have enjoyed the calm happiness of the hearth. Like Michel, she lacks, as Gide noted in the *Journal des Faux-Monnayeurs*, "the bit of good sense which keeps me from pushing their [the characters'] follies as far as they do." But Alissa lacks even more: beneath her intense piety she has a need to sublimate her fears and intensities into safe and traditionally respected channels. By striving for sanctity, she avoids having to create a personality of her own and to deal with instincts she fears are hers.

La Porte étroite is divided into two parts or, rather, it is composed of two *récits:* Jerome's narrative of events and Alissa's record of her reactions in her journal. Although in reality they represent two independent *récits*, the second narrative, along with Alissa's dialogues and letters quoted in the first part, is by far the more interesting and more important. Jerome's narrative exists only as a preparation and contextual explanation for the spiritual evolution traced in Alissa's journal. Jerome comes off as a rather docile and dependent man in whose literary style is reflected the hesitation, self-righteousness, and fondness for constant qualifications of the character. His style is flaccid, picky, Gide said on several occasions, but it is necessarily so. Jerome's narrative puts Alissa's journal and personality in relief by sparing her the need to recount facts and events that would normally weaken the intensity of her emotions and character development. Jerome acts as a possible and ever-ready solution to her dilemma but leaves any decision entirely up to her. His constancy and passivity are part of the décor in Alissa's world and exert upon her no pressure which she cannot easily combat.

Several other characters model for her the consequences of Jerome's offer. Tante Plantier, fertile, buxom, and devoted to her issue, as well as to that of her family, offers earthy wit, wisdom, and sound advice. Alissa's sister, Juliette, also counsels a less stringent path and acts upon her beliefs. Rather than waste her life pining for Jerome, with whom, unbelievably, she is in love, she attempts by force of will to balance her needs and the possibilities of satisfying them. She marries another and settles down to some semblance of happiness.

After her sister's marriage, Alissa finds herself facing a still available Jerome and persists in not yielding. "An absolutely useless heroism," Gide said about her resistance. "The thought of her fiancé invoked in her, immediately, a sort of flush of heroism, that was not voluntary, but practically unconscious, irresistible and spontaneous." But this heroism is not entirely gratuitous. Jerome's presence immediately calls into play Alissa's sense of her own virtue, which is as strong as she fears her propensity to vice demands. In the closely knit world circumscribed by their families and the Protestant parish, only Alissa's mother, Lucile Bucolin, is an intruder. A Creole by birth and a courtesan by temperament, she flaunts herself with great glee in the ascetic environment she married into. While her children are still young and impressionable, she obtrusively takes a lover and finally disappears with him. It is apropos of this tragedy that the local pastor plants the justification of Alissa's and Jerome's withdrawal from life in a sermon based on Christ's words: "Strive to enter through the narrow gate" (Luke, XIII:24). Sensitive to what she fears she inherited from her mother, and aware that she resembles her greatly, Alissa early chooses to develop only the spiritual side of her nature, to which she directs all her intensity.

Alissa's choice of the narrow path is also strengthened by the numerous dead-end paths traced by those around her: examples of her unhappy father, of Jerome's widowed mother forever dressed in mourning, and of her lifelong companion, Miss Flora Ashburton, all encourage her to take any involvement other than spiritual as weakness or vice. But she is also trapped by a weak Jerome. Instead of helping her integrate conflicting elements in her personality with his protection and understanding, he follows her lead and plays her game. "It is by being infatuated with his own weakness that man imitates," Ménalque tells Michel in a line eventually deleted from *L'Immoraliste*. In Alissa's case, it is through fear that she imitates the asceticism prevalent in her milieu and it is because her intensity is frustrated by Jerome's weakness that she strives to realize what she feels is her noblest part by developing it to its extreme in death.

La Symphonie pastorale (1919) is, like the other *récits*, an ironic book. It criticizes self-deception in a form to which Gide himself was particularly vulnerable: liberally interpreting the Scriptures to suit one's own needs and weaknesses. The pastor of La Brévine, a small mountain village in the Swiss Jura, recounts the development and education of a blind fifteen-year-old girl he had found two and one-half years earlier. Though not deaf, his young charge spent her first years in total silence and darkness because her aunt, whose death provided the occasion for the pastor's recovery of the child, was deaf herself. Moved by feelings of charity, the pastor decides to undertake the salvation of this soul lost in darkness, at great moral and physical expense to his wife and his own children. He soothes his disgruntled wife with arguments of charity and promises of help, although, in truth, his first impulse was to cite some of Christ's words. "I kept them back, however, because it seems to me improper to cover my behavior behind the authority of the Holy Scriptures." But this is precisely what he does, increasingly and heedlessly, throughout the book. Moreover, as his wife seems to become more and more peevish toward him, and as his own children interest him less, he becomes withdrawn and dependent upon himself to satisfy his intellectual, emotional, and spiritual needs. Because Gertrude, as he calls his charge, needs constant, patient attention and because she proves intelligent and responsive, he begins to fashion her as a complement to his own soul. Like an aging André Walter, he hopes to form the soul of his beloved so like his own that nothing can separate them. But soon love and charity change into something less generous and more earthy. When his wife chides him for spending more time with Gertrude than he ever spent with his own children, he hides behind the parable of the lost sheep. The more intense he becomes, the greater grows his dependence upon the Gospels as sanctions.

But his dependence is selective. In the second notebook, where the narrative structure yields to day-by-day journal entries, he immediately confesses his discovery of his true feelings after having reread his story. He had not previously realized that love was in question because he had felt no guilt. It is a small step, then, to defend the innocence of those feelings, and it is a step he takes blithely. The second entry of the notebook is laden with irony:

Gertrude's religious instruction has made me reread the Evangile with new eyes. It is more and more apparent to me that a number of notions which make up our Christian faith stem not from Christ's words but from St. Paul's commentaries.

He proceeds to reconstruct standards of guilt by defining evil as any obstacle to happiness. The Gospels, he feels, teach principally "a method for attaining a life of happiness." The pastor concludes, "Gertrude's complete happiness, which shines out from her whole being, comes from her ignorance of sin." Moral strictures, he argues, invoking part of Romans XIV, are dictated not by law but by love: "Nothing is unclean in itself; but it is unclean for anyone who thinks it unclean" (XIV:14).

[26]

Gertrude's education makes her, in effect, a creature living in an illusory world of goodness, beauty, and eternal happiness. Into this world of harmony, indeed a pastoral symphony in its own way, the pastor allows no intrusion of reality. He rejects his son's interest in Gertrude and forbids him from courting her, going so far as to accuse him of wanting to "take advantage of a disabled, innocent, and guileless person." When he is finally convinced of his son's honorable intentions, he can only ask for more time to think of a valid opposition to his son's proposed plans. "An instinct as sure as the voice of conscience warned me that I had to prevent this marriage at all costs." Later called upon to explain his reasons, he admits that he followed his conscience and not his reason, invoking Gertrude's innocence, impressionability, and lack of prudence. "It is a question of conscience," he concludes lamely.

Since even here the standard of judgment is his own conscience, his task is to ease this conscience. He immediately takes communion, surprisingly unattended at the altar by either his wife or son. The latter's abstention is clarified by the subsequent entries in the second notebook and puts into relief the exegetical clash that long interested Gide. His son, the pastor believes, feels doomed as soon as he discovers himself without props or authority to guide him. But Jacques insists upon facing the ever-present reality of sin, evil, and death by supporting St. Paul and accepting the necessity of commandments, threats, and prohibition. "In submission lies happiness," he says and quotes a verse from Romans that his father had curiously overlooked earlier: "Do not let what you eat cause the ruin of one for whom Christ died" (XIV:15). The pastor remains absolutely impervious to the meaning of this verse by claiming fidelity to Christ and not to St. Paul; he is closer to Christ when he teaches that sin is only what disrupts the happiness of another "or compromises our very own." The example of his father, Jacques admits late in the book, has in fact, guided him to understand the wisdom of converting to Catholicism.

Gertrude herself senses the incompleteness of the world picture offered her by the pastor. In a tender scene near the end of the book, she acknowledges that her happiness seems to be based on ignorance. She would prefer lucidity to happiness, would prefer knowing what evil and ugliness there is about her just to be sure that she is not adding any of her own. The subsequent conversation suggests what she has on her mind; she wants reassurance from him that her children will not inherit her blindness, that their love is real and passionate, although guilty. Finally, she admits that she ought to feel guilty but that she cannot stop loving him. The pastor cannot respond, cannot reassure her one way or the other, cannot do more than wallow in his own lightheadedness. He is now thoroughly prepared to do what he feared Jacques had in mind, to take advantage of weakness, innocence, and ignorance.

The discovery that Gertrude's sight can be restored acts as a catalyst. Unable to refuse to do what for Gertrude must be a boon, still he is reluctant to break the news to her. On several occasions he tries and fails until finally he finds himself alone with her in her room: "I held her close to me for some time. She made no move to resist and, as she raised her face toward mine, our lips met."

She enters the hospital the following day. After a successful operation and convalescence, she returns home and attempts suicide. When she sees the family, and especially Amélie, the wife, she realizes immediately that she had usurped the place of another; she sees her sin, her error. Now thoroughly familiar with St. Paul, thanks to Jacques's company during her convalescence, she quotes Romans VII:9: "I was once alive apart from the law, but when the commandment came sin revived and I died." She dies, in fact, shortly after with a reproach on her lips: having seen Jacques she realized that it was he whom she loved, and that it was he whom she could have married were it not for the pastor. Jacques, on the other hand, follows through to the end the path diametrically opposite to his father's: he accepts orthodoxy and converts himself and Gertrude to Catholicism. Like Michel, the pastor, though with different emphases, if not different motives, refuses, at least in theory, to acknowledge any authority other than his own conscience, a conscience he claims to be thoroughly grounded in the words and example of Christ. In practice, however, he constantly passes off responsibility onto God, Christ, or the Scriptures, finding what he deems authorization for his own passion.

Les Faux-Monnayeurs (1926), the first and only book of his Gide dared call a novel, had so long been on his mind that when he began writing it, in June, 1919, he decided to record his progress in a special logbook, *Le Journal des Faux-Monnayeurs*. His timidity and reluctance with regard to the term "novel" can be explained by the rigor of his concept of the genre. The novel, for Gide, must of necessity present reality as seen from multiple vantage points, must suggest the profusion and formlessness of the real world, while at the same time demonstrating a number of attempts to come to grips with it either artistically, psychologically, socially, or philosophically, and all interacting with one another. The first *sotie* and the *récits* present, at most, no more than two points of view whose purity of development is not hindered by any external pressures. The main concern in these works is essentially the interior world of the protagonist, hence, the first-person narrative. With *Les Caves* Gide begins to show an interest in the reciprocal influences of the interior and exterior worlds of a number of protagonists each in conflict with another. Its relation with the more sober *Faux-Monnayeurs* is attested to by Gide's long-standing intention to use Lafcadio as a principal character of the later book; but even more convincing is the absolute identity of tone between the *sotie* and several chapters of the novel recounted in the third person. Particularly revealing is the second chapter in which the two magistrates, Oscar Molinier and Albéric Profitendieu, stroll home at competitive paces and, puppet-like, parade for one another personalities atrophied not so much by their profession as by their own image of themselves. Both are as much caricatures as Anthime Armand-Dubois or Amédée Fleurissoire.

Significant, too, is the omniscient third-person narrative device used rarely by Gide though insistently in both *Les Caves du Vatican* and *Les Faux-Monnayeurs*. But in the latter, the omniscient author surpasses the role of a technique or device: he himself becomes a character in the story he has invented not only by reacting to and commenting upon his people but also by illustrating still another "point of view" and still another attempt, albeit successful, to make something of reality, to make a book out of the material the world offers. Like the omniscient author, Edouard is writing a novel also called *Les Faux-Monnayeurs* and keeping a journal in which he notes all that can be of use for his book. Here he faces the same problems in handling events suggested by Gide and the omniscient author he plays. Finally, through letters, but mostly through dialogue reported either by the omniscient author or by Edouard, Gide succeeds in presenting still more points of view and efforts at fashioning a viable approach to reality.

In the novel, then, a number of people speak for themselves and reveal their efforts to reconcile themselves somehow to the world about them. Some have already erected a workable system and have settled themselves in it; for the most part these are the older generation: the magistrates; the pastors Azaïs and Vedel, who are Parisian transplants of the pastor of *La Symphonie pastorale;* La Pérouse, who is painfully discovering the cruel trick God has played on him; Passavant, who, like Barag-lioul, plays to the crowd; even Pauline Molinier, who spends a better part of her life covering up the inadequacies and hypoc-risy of her husband. For the most part, adolescents or young adults, that is, those undergoing the dynamic processes of "becoming," understandably attract and retain most of the narrator's and Edouard's attention. And still a third group finds a voice in the novel: the young teen-agers who are not so much struggling with the real world at large as with the imme-diate social and cultural influences they are undergoing: Boris, Georges, Ghérandisol, and the vaguely suggested Caloub.

These three groups represent not only three major age divi-sions but more significantly three stages in the struggle between atrophy and plenitude or, in terms consistent with the novel's central image scheme, between authenticity and the counter-feit. The profound subject of the novel is precisely the many alternatives people choose with which to face the world, alter-natives which are completely external to their personality and based on convention, revolt, or a simple lack of common sense. Gide's *Faux-Monnayeurs* is, in fact, a catalogue of the various ways in which one can live a counterfeit life—but, especially, it is a catalogue of the various pressures which tend to divert those striving for plenitude.

In the very center of the novel two significant events take place: Edouard discusses the theory of the novel in general and of his own in particular, and Bernard uncovers a counterfeit coin. The two events are intimately related, especially in regard to the development of Edouard's character. One of his inter-locutors finally asks him exactly who are the counterfeiters he proposes to write about. Like his predecessor, the narrator of *Paludes*, Edouard gets tangled up in the exposition of ideas too close to him and in the description of work in progress. The bad impression he makes upon his friends is only partially atoned for by the narrator's intrusion and explanation of Edouard's thought. Edouard's use of the counterfeiters is purely figurative, we learn. At first the term designated certain of his colleagues.

But the attribution broadened considerably; according as the wind of the spirit blew from Rome or elsewhere, his heroes became either priests or freemasons. If he let his mind go its way, it would soon capsize in abstraction where it would wallow comfortably. Ideas of exchange, devaluation, inflation were little by little over-running his book as did theories of dress in Carlyle's *Sartor Resartus* where they usurped the characters' roles.

Though the title of *Les Faux-Monnayeurs* refers to something quite concrete, Edouard thinks of it in figurative and abstract terms. And it is precisely this that his young secretary Bernard objects to. Bernard shows him a false 10-franc piece and urges him to begin not with the idea of the counterfeit but with a fact, a false 10-franc coin, for example. He forces him to admit that such reality, although it does indeed interest him, basically troubles him. In fact, so deep is this trouble that only his diary, and the processes of articulation it requires, can give any semblance of reality to whatever happens to him. Or at least so he rationalizes in his journal. But he goes on to demonstrate a case in point. Recording the thoughts provoked by the false coin and his subsequent discussion with Bernard, he realizes that we create the drama of our lives by our attempt to impose upon the world our interpretation of it and by the way it resists.

The resistance of facts invites us to transpose our ideal construction onto the world of dreams, of hope, of future life in which our belief is nourished by all our failures in this one. Realists begin with facts and adjust their ideas to them. Bernard is a realist. I am afraid I won't be able to get along with him.

That is, unlike Bernard, he will not adjust himself to facts but will adjust them, in his novel and journal, to fit his own ideas.

With this admission, Edouard unwittingly classifies himself among the counterfeiters. Like Azaïs, the old pastor, and his son-in-law, Vedel, Edouard has constructed a world for himself frequently unencumbered either by fact or by reality. But even Edouard changes and leaves us with a slight hope: finally settled in a satisfactory relationship with his nephew, Olivier, he manages to write the first thirty pages of his novel.

However ambiguous Edouard's own status might appear by the end of the novel, that of most others in flux throughout the novel seems clear. Those who had reached the final stage of development at the opening have failed and live counterfeit lives. What is worse, however, is that they persist in their error and force those around them either to imitate them or to reject their error in favor of an extreme just as false. The old pastor, Azaïs, because of his fervor, sincerity, and simplicity, forces those he faces into playing a role, acquiescing and being hypocrites as soon as they feel unable to share his convictions and enthusiasms. The hypocrisy of his son-in-law, Vedel, who continues to affect piety and devotion out of fidelity to an early enthusiasm, thickens the atmosphere of lies that his children have to grow up in. They are all pushed into making some sort of stand with regard to their upbringing: most of the children rebel and cynically project their rebellion into an ethic. An unnamed son leaves for Africa when he feels he cannot handle the rumblings of puberty; Laura goes off to England, marries a colorless French professor, commits adultery, and finds herself bearing her lover's child; Sarah ultimately goes off to England, thus proclaiming her independence after having exercised it promiscuously under the very nose of familial authority; Armand, sensitive and troubled, becomes intellectually promiscuous and establishes cynicism and hypocrisy as the tenets of his ethic. Rachel alone stays at home; through total self-effacement she undertakes to deal with all the realities her

[33]

father and grandfather do not acknowledge by keeping the household financially solvent.

Laura, after a bad start, seems to be heading toward a better future: she returns to her husband who forgives all and promises to treat the child as his own. Albéric Profitendieu under similar circumstances made a similar promise to Marguerite some nineteen years earlier. When Bernard discovers to his great relief that Profitendieu is not his real father and that he will not have the problem of rejecting or accepting the centripetal forces of heredity and early upbringing, he runs away from home seeking adventures which will enable him better to gauge his true potential. Like Michel, he dares free himself and follow his bent. Unlike his predecessor, however, he enters into a long struggle with himself from which he emerges, if not victorious, at least a bit more matured and endowed with that grain of good sense that so many of Gide's characters lack. Unlike Lafcadio, too, he learns that in this world it is not enough to dare. "He was beginning to understand that other people's happiness is often the price of daring." Learning that Profitendieu is alone and ailing, he returns home, not out of weakness, but out of the affection he had always felt for the man he had long taken for his father; he returns, too, because he has gained a feeling of freedom so profound that it frees him from the constant need to test and prove it. With Bernard and Laura, Olivier Molinier also promises to develop in the direction of authenticity. Unlike his brothers, he manages to escape the baneful influence of his complacent and hypocritical father and his well-meaning though no less hypocritical mother. Adopted by Edouard, his uncle, Olivier will live in an open atmosphere that will permit him to develop fully.

As sensitive and intelligent as his younger brother Olivier, Vincent Molinier falls into Michel's trap of illusory self-development and freedom. He seduces and then abandons Laura, is seduced, in turn, by Lady Griffith, exalts himself and her by exercising his will and strength, destroying first his more noble and generous instincts and finally his mistress herself. He abandons himself to his instincts, ignorant of the proviso in Edouard's often quoted formula: "It is good to follow your bent, provided it moves upwards." Georges Molinier, though still a teen-ager, seems at first to have chosen the way of revolt and defiance. Like his classmate Ghérandisol, nephew and pro-tégé of the novel's Protos-like figure, Strouvilhou, Georges is in the process of fashioning himself into a "subtle one" and inadvertently falls into a system as rigid as the one he would escape. Through a suicide pact reserved only for a select few in their class, he and Ghérandisol provoke the suicide of another classmate, the timid and tormented grandson of La Pérouse, Boris. It is only with great effort that he finally comes to his senses and seeks the help of his mother. Ghérandisol, on the other hand, regrets only having lost his *sang-froid* by uncontrollably shuddering at the sight of the cadaver.

Boris is a victim not only of his classmate's cruelty but also of his temperament, his early upbringing, and especially of Sophroniska, a sort of Freudian analyst into whose care Boris has been entrusted. Rigorously following certain psychoanalytical theories, Sophroniska so deforms facts to fit her interpretation of reality that she cannot realize the true causes of Boris' emotional improvement. Of far greater effectiveness for the young boy than her theories is the idyllic relationship between her charge and her daughter, Bronja.

In this one book, into which Gide wanted to pour all that life had shown and taught him, we find a catalogue of various types of counterfeit personalities and of the influences which force them to forsake authenticity. Essentially, the book is a study of the adolescent personality in its struggle and growth toward a full or atrophied maturity. But the book also contains aesthetic theories of fiction in the process of maturing in Edouard's mind and balanced against the logbook of Gide's own theories. Gide put much of his thought into the mouth of Edouard; but the latter frequently develops his ideas to a point beyond logic or refuses to anchor them in reality. Reality bothers him, he tells Bernard during the long discussion of the novel, and for this very reason Bernard is quick to suggest that, in his book, Edouard begin right off with facts, with the counterfeit coins. Although Bernard, the realist, introduces the false coins only at the end of the second part, and the intrigue is clarified only in Part Three, postponing these real facts forces them to act as concrete catalysts in a rather abstract system. As Edouard thinks first of the counterfeit only in a figurative sense, so, too, Gide's novel presents a series of people either living a lie or in the process of struggling with one. But these are viewed as counterfeit, that is, they earn the counterfeit label, only when the reality of the counterfeit coins intrudes itself upon the orderly world of the novel. Similarly, the brutality of Boris' death intrudes itself upon Edouard's consciousness and perception of the world.

That is why I will not use Boris' suicide in my Faux-Monnayeurs; I already have enough difficulty understanding it. And, then, I don't like "news items." They have in them a bit of the peremptory, the undeniable, the brutal, the outrageously real. . . . I allow reality to support my thought as a proof; but not to precede it. I don't like being surprised. I see Boris' suicide as an indecency because I didn't expect it.

Boris' grandfather, La Pérouse, cannot assimilate this event either; plunged in a mystical despair which makes of man the victim of a unified God and Satan, he cannot express his sorrow directly, a sorrow too profound, too "astounding," as Edouard observes, "to allow any steady contemplation."

After *Les Faux-Monnayeurs*, Gide wrote nothing of the stature of his previous fiction unless it be *Thésée*. One can easily suppose that he literally used himself up on his novel just as he had foreseen in the *Journal des Faux-Monnayeurs*. As he suggests on several occasions in his journal, were it not for an "undeniable diminution" in his creative prowess, his interest in social problems and in communism (1926–36) would not have usurped the place of his personal, moral concerns. But the lessening of his creative powers during the thirties can be even further explained from another vantage point. Nearly all of his books up to and including *Les Faux-Monnayeurs* answered a profound psychological need. The work of art provided him with a crutch thanks to which he was able to achieve "an equilibrium beyond time, an artificial health" that he felt totally incapable of achieving *in vivo*. But as he grew older and more and more reconciled to his anomaly, the stability obtained by composing works of art was slowly and imperceptibly transferred onto his person; he began to live maintaining a balance of the various contradictory forces of his personality. If, as Gide so often claimed, the spur of every social reform is an anomaly, an imbalance, a potential atrophy, his own deep-rooted perplexities dissolved as he exorcised the tyrannical potential of each of them. As he became well adjusted, he lost all desire to repeat reforms he had already worked out: by 1926 he had written a catharsis of asceticism, of hedonism, and of a sort of romantic imagination; he had written a defense of homosexuality, a case study of himself, in the form of memoirs, as well as the long-dreamed-of *summa*, *Les Faux-Monnayeurs*.

In a journal entry for July 19, 1932, Gide stated, "each of my books has, up until now, focused upon an uncertainty." A glance back at his works up to *Les Faux-Monnayeurs* bears out the basic validity of this insight; supporting it, too, are the many statements Gide made in the *Journal* and elsewhere concerning the answers each of his works provided for inner needs. In his attempt to achieve a fuller life, without the inhibiting consequences of real action, Gide relied upon his fantasy and made his protagonists act out to the fullest extent possible each of his own temptations. This explains the compensatory violence of a book like *Les Nourritures terrestres* (1897) produced at the beginning of his career and certainly representing an epoch-making statement in the Gidian canon. And, too, why in 1927 Gide brought this book out of limbo and republished it; finally, why in 1935, at the peak of his political fervor, he returned to this format and published *Les Nouvelles nourritures.*

As Gide knew long before he wrote the 1927 preface, *Les Nourritures terrestres* was a book of convalescence, the fruit, as he said to Christian Beck in 1907, of his tuberculosis. "There is in its very lyricism, the excesses of one who clutches life as something he has almost lost." The scope of this statement should be extended to include the excesses of him who embraces life as something he had long denied himself. There is no fanatic like a new convert and Gide consciously exorcised the extremes of hedonism, of fanaticism in his song on the fruits of the earth. Conscious of the efficacy and psychic stability provided by a "system of compensations," and of the "usefulness of illness," as he noted in 1896 (*Journal*, I, 98), he abandoned himself to the eulogy of fervor, freedom, and joy. In abandoning himself—at least literarily—he both compensated for the effects of a cloistered youth and adolescence and let these "safe" compensations run their course. In this way he expended his hedonism but he did not abandon his theory; he continued to praise the fruits of the earth and urged his disciple Nathanaël, no less strongly at the end than at the beginning, to go his way alone, to rely on no one and nothing outside himself, to the point, even, of abandoning his master and this "manual of evasion."

Les Nourritures terrestres has been taken most frequently as a eulogy of hedonism. It is true that those who speak in the "essay" tell of joy encountered and appetites satisfied, but the tone of voice in all cases is unique and the same. Essentially, it is a hortatory tone, with Ménalque inviting his listeners, the narrator urging his readers and, especially, his young disciple, Nathanaël, to feed upon the fruits of the earth. In a very real sense, then, *Les Nourritures terrestres*, like an antidote to *Paludes*, represents the aspirations of a long-sheltered and ascetic youth toward a full earthly experience and, ultimately, toward an equilibrium between the pleasures of the senses and those of the soul. But for the young Huguenot even pure hedonism was not easy to achieve without the essential condition so difficult for an introspective intellectual: the suppression of his thought and attendant self-consciousness.

It is not surprising that the narrator feels obliged to reject speaking of himself, to defer the "ballad on the different forms of the mind," and to state, "Have you noticed that there is *no one* in this book? And even I am no more than vision in it." Similarly, in the 1927 preface, Gide felt it necessary to point out that rather than hedonism his book glorifies destitution and, primarily, stripping oneself of one's ever-hovering intellect. In almost the same way as Gide condemned his own thought on a number of occasions, Ménalque in Book IV chides a comrade who has wife, children, books, and a study, for expecting "to savor the powerful, total, and immediate sensation of life without forgetting what is extraneous to it. Your habit of thinking is a burden to you; you live either in the past or the future and you perceive nothing spontaneously. We are nothing except in the instantaneity of life; the entire past dies in it before anything yet to come is born." And this Ménalque affirms after recounting how at fifty he sold "absolutely everything, not wanting to retain anything *personal* on earth; not even the slightest memory of yesteryear."

[39]

Book IV, which is nearly entirely devoted to Ménalque's autobiography, picks up and repeats the ideas and themes carefully suggested and developed in the first three books. The central idea developed by Ménalque revolves about his aversion to possessions of any kind for fear of possessing no more than that. Such a fear of property originally kept him from making any choices and, ultimately, from undertaking any action at all. But he finally sees the light and understands that "all the drops from this vast divine source are equivalent; that the tiniest suffices to intoxicate us and to reveal the plenitude and totality of God." In effect, destitution provokes our thirst and hunger, incites our fervor, and enables us to receive and enjoy anything in our path. Ménalque rejects everything that might inhibit his receptivity to all sensations in their force and immediacy: he rejects family, institutions, hopes for the future, reliance on the past, everything but the slow, deliberate, and random cultivation of all his senses. He rejects, too, anything that stops challenging him to find and deploy new strengths; when people and things become familiar, he feels, they breed repose and reliance on past accomplishment. It is in this spirit that he concludes: "My heart without any attachment on earth has remained poor, and I will die easily. My happiness is made of fervor. Through all things indistinctly, I have adored intensely."

Fancy is bred not in the eye but in the mind, and therein lies the flaw in Gide's book and its ethics, a flaw he was well aware of and which he casually exploits in the book itself. For fervor must be maintained at any price and by any means if the intensity of sensations is to continue as a cultivation of the self. This movement from the search for experience to the search for sensations and for ever-new sensations capable of maintaining fervor eventually degenerates to a frenzied hunt for stimulation. Finally there obtains a loss of the self so complete, a self so detached from past and future that the narrator feels possessed. "What is called 'meditation' is an impossible constraint for me; I no longer understand the word 'solitude'; to be alone with myself is to be no longer anyone; I am inhabited."

In a letter to Marcel Drouin Gide said that he was concerned in *Les Nourritures* only with one side of the coin, with the joy of desire and not the anguish and dissolution that it causes. But this in no way implies he was unaware of the other side; he would deal with it later, contenting himself for the moment by suggesting in the later books of *Les Nourritures* possible outcomes of Ménalque's doctrine that call to mind *Saül* (1903) and *L'Immoraliste*. He felt that the importance of *Les Nourritures* lay precisely in the full and unfettered exploitation of the sensual side of his personality. Letting it run its course, at least in the work of art, brought him to several other conclusions he later was able to verify *in vivo*. In *Le Renoncement au voyage* (1906), Gide realized that his hypersensitivity stemmed mostly from his thirst so long repressed and not from a permanent physiological state. You cannot go back and find the same intensity of a former naïve self, Gide says during his sixth visit to North Africa. And even in Book VIII of *Les Nourritures*, the narrator nostalgically states the difficulty of becoming once again the young man he was in Biskra: "He who I was, that *other* one, ah! how could I become him again?"

Thus even in *Les Nourritures*, where Gide planned to sing the joys of the flesh and fruits of the earth, in compensation for the austere and cerebral side of his nature, he could not but indicate the deformed figure such an ethic can produce and by contrast suggest the ideal of equilibrium and plenitude. Here, already, are prefigurations of Michel and Saül, both dispossessed by the will-eroding power of their desires. And, at last, even in his last *récit*, the long happy life of Theseus, which he recounts with a measure of satisfaction and an abundance of detail, Gide cannot help confronting his pragmatic hero with the suffering and inspired Oedipus.

The long road traveled by Gide in search of tranquillity and plenitude is dramatically illustrated by the juxtaposition of these two books, *Les Nourritures terrestres* and *Thésée* (1946): the one, an initial Dionysiac plunge into sensation doubled by a vague hesitation and anticipation of disaster, and the other, no less intense sensually but set in balance by a taut springlike will power, a Cornelian sense of duty and service, and a devotion to a balanced exploitation of all his strengths. Theseus is a child of this earth, agile physically, intellectually, and emotionally; socially and sexually wily and adept, yet less given to indulgence of his pleasure than of his strengths and virtues.

The first great lesson Theseus recalls in his memoirs is a reliance on reason, and the second, an exercise in strengthening his will. His father, Aegeus, one day told him that his pastoral life would soon have to come to an end: he was a king's son and would have to become worthy of succeeding his father on the throne. By a ruse, claiming that special weapons for Theseus were hidden by Poseidon beneath a stone, Aegeus succeeds in building up both Theseus' moral and physical strength; in his determination to find the weapons Theseus leaves no stone unturned, beginning even to tear apart the palace terrace. Aegeus gives his arms to Theseus, feeling that his son has amply shown a desire for glory which will not permit them to be used for any but noble ends and mankind's happiness. In this manner Theseus developed an ethic that enabled him to overcome many monsters both within and without his personality; he strengthened his will, enabling him to "stop living with abandon, however pleasing this freedom might have been." Though always ready for pleasure and never refusing to savor an amorous exploit, he never let himself be saddled by one and quickly went beyond them; in love, as in all else, "I was always less concerned and withheld by what I had accomplished than pulled by what still had to be done; and the more important always seemed to me still to come."

Theseus suggests that the exceptional person is the one with an exceptionally strong will, the strength of which enables him to transcend the normal limits of good and evil and, for the greater glory of himself and future generations, to do, in fact, no evil . . . or, at least, to compensate for it. He embodies Gide's ethic in a curiously neo-Leibnitzian form: what is, is good, and what the hero does is good. A constant control and assurance is provided by his sense of duty and the full exploitation of his strengths and aptitudes. The hero ever strives to integrate within his experience the largest possible segment of reality about him, with its and his harmonies and dissonances.

The basis of the *récit* is built around a series of great encounters from which Theseus derives some personal benefit: two chapters are devoted to his early life and to the formative influences of his father and grandfather; eight chapters are devoted to Theseus' stay in Knossos, his encounters with Daedalus, Minos and his family, particularly Ariadne, Phaedra, and the Minotaur; the final chapters revolve about the flight from Crete, the founding of Athens; finally, in an epilogue, Gide confronts Oedipus with Theseus.

The confrontations with Daedalus and later with Oedipus are the key chapters of the narrative. As architect of the labyrinth, Daedalus is especially qualified to explain the subtle nature of his prison as well as to provide Theseus with a plan enabling him to enter the maze, accomplish his deed, and escape with little difficulty. To detain people in his labyrinth, Daedalus explains, it would be more effective to design a structure from which people would not want to escape. With this in mind, he fills the hallways and rooms of the maze with appetizers, incenses, and gases of all sorts that act upon the will. "Each

person, following the inclination his own mind thereupon pre-
pares, loses himself, if you will, in his own private labyrinth."

The way to overcome these subtle narcotics is to maintain
a taut will, support it with a homemade gas mask, and guide
oneself with reels of thread, firmly anchored outside the labyrinth. Daedalus calls this thread "a tangible symbol of duty,"
and says it is Theseus' bond to his past and to his future; for
without it, his life would become a hopeless imbroglio and a
permanent immersion in the present and in the presence of
sensations.

In the last encounter at Colonus both Theseus and Oedipus
measure themselves against one another. By beginning the epilogue with an account of his own suffering, Theseus attempts
to equate himself with Oedipus. Only in this area does there
seem to be a common ground between the two. For Theseus
had succeeded in all he had undertaken, whereas Oedipus had
failed. "His misfortunes," Theseus writes, "could only enhance
his grandeur in my eyes. No doubt I had triumphed every-
where and always, but on a level which, in comparison with
Oedipus, seemed to me merely human, inferior, I might say."
Here for the first time Theseus catches a glimpse of the infinite
and has difficulty understanding. Why had Oedipus accepted
defeat by putting out his eyes? Had he not even contributed
to it? Oedipus gropes around for an answer likely to reach his
interlocutor and convey some sort of meaning to him. He says
he put out his eyes to punish them for not having seen the
obvious, as an instinctive gesture, as an attempt to see his des-
tiny through to the very end, or to destroy the false picture of
the world of appearances in the hope of seeing into the "real,
insensible" world beyond that is the realm of God. Theseus
admits he does not quite fathom these explanations but does
not deny the importance the spiritual world might have for

some; but he cannot accept the opposition Oedipus sets up between their two worlds. Like most of the book, in fact, Theseus' incomprehension and, then, final acceptance of Oedipus on Attic territory are the fruit of his constant attempt to contain all extremes and maintain them in equilibrium.

Like Theseus, Gide attempted to take into account as much of the world and as many ways of approaching it as possible. Theseus might not understand Oedipus' mystical impulse but he certainly does make place for it, as he makes place for Oedipus in his realms. So, too, Gide himself; but he goes beyond each of his characters by balancing within himself both transcendental and terrestrial values.

And this attitude is evident in his memoirs, his journal, his travelogues, and especially in his criticism where it becomes an aesthetic criterion. He saw himself as a modern counterpart to the classicists in whom he valued above all else their modesty and its artistic analogue, litotes; their striving to take into account and maintain in harmony as much of reality as possible, and to express the totality of their age. The limits of art, he said in an important lecture in 1901, like the limits of the human personality, are not external or legislatable but exist within the artist and within the human being. And as such, they are not simply separate extremes but limits of a continuous extension. That is, Gide clarifies by quoting Pascal, "one does not know one's greatness by being at one extremity, but by touching both at the same time and filling in between them." Echoing this notion in the *Journal* of 1930, Gide remarks flippantly that he is ever conscious of his limits because he never occupies the center of his cage: "My whole being rushes toward the bars." The conclusion of the lecture rephrases an idea very dear to Gide: the artist must submit "to himself as much as possible, as much of nature as possible." This rewords an earlier idea

[45]

often repeated in the *Journal* and elsewhere that Gide reprinted in capitals in *Les Nourritures:* "Take to oneself as much humanity as possible."

Gide's unending search for harmony, for an equilibrium, attainable only with difficulty for it to have any value, lies at the heart of his ethic and aesthetic: works of different types, developing character traits to their extreme, represent less an exclusion by catharsis than an attempt to integrate these traits in the context of his whole personality. "Let's integrate, then," he tells his imaginary correspondent, Angèle, in a letter on classicism (1921). "Let's integrate. All that classicism refuses to integrate just might turn against it."

SELECTED BIBLIOGRAPHY

PRINCIPAL WORKS OF ANDRÉ GIDE

Les Cahiers d'André Walter. Paris, Librairie de l'Art Indépendant, 1891. ("Le Cahier blanc," Part 1, The White Notebook. Tr. with an introduction by Wade Baskin. New York, Citadel Press, 1965.)

Le Traité du Narcisse. Paris, Librairie de l'Art Indépendant, 1891.

La Tentative amoureuse. Paris, Librairie de l'Art Indépendant, 1893.

Le Voyage d'Urien. Paris, Librairie de l'Art Indépendant, 1893. (Urien's Voyage. Tr. with an introduction by Wade Baskin. New York, Citadel Press, 1964.)

Paludes. Paris, Librairie de l'Art Indépendant, 1895. (Marshlands, and Prometheus Misbound: Two Satires. Tr. George D. Painter. New York, New Directions, 1953.)

Les Nourritures terrestres. Paris, Mercure de France, 1897. (The Fruits of the Earth. Tr. Dorothy Bussy. New York, Alfred A. Knopf, 1949.)

Le Prométhée mal enchaîné. Paris, Mercure de France, 1899. (Marshlands, and Prometheus Misbound: Two Satires. Tr. George D. Painter. New York, New Directions, 1953.)

L'Immoraliste. Paris, Mercure de France, 1902. (The Immoralist. Tr. Dorothy Bussy. New York, Alfred A. Knopf, 1930.)

La Porte étroite. Paris, Mercure de France, 1909. (Strait Is the Gate. Tr. Dorothy Bussy. New York, Alfred A. Knopf, 1924.)

Isabelle. Paris, Gallimard, 1911. (Isabelle, in Two Symphonies. Tr. Dorothy Bussy. New York, Alfred A. Knopf, 1931.)

Les Caves du Vatican. Paris, Gallimard, 1914. (The Vatican Swindle. Tr. Dorothy Bussy. New York, Alfred A. Knopf, 1925. Also issued under title Lafcadio's Adventures. New York, Alfred A. Knopf, 1927.)

La Symphonie pastorale. Paris, Gallimard, 1919. (The Pastoral Symphony, in Two Symphonies. Tr. Dorothy Bussy. New York, Alfred A. Knopf, 1931.)

Les Faux-Monnayeurs. Paris, Gallimard, 1926. (The Counterfeiters. Tr. Dorothy Bussy. New York, Alfred A. Knopf, 1927.)

Journal des Faux-Monnayeurs. Paris, Gallimard, 1926. (Journal of the Counterfeiters. Tr. Justin O'Brien. Included in The Counterfeiters.)

Si le grain ne meurt. Paris, Gallimard, 1926. (If It Die. Tr. Dorothy Bussy. New York, Random House, 1935.)

Oedipe. Paris, 1931. (Oedipus, in Two Legends: Oedipus and Theseus. Tr. John Russell. New York, Alfred A. Knopf, 1950.)

Journal, 1889–1949. Souvenirs. Bibliothèque de la Pléiade. 2 vols. Paris, Gallimard, 1948, 1954. (The Journals of André Gide. Tr. Justin O'Brien. 4 vols. New York, Alfred A. Knopf, 1947–51.)

Théâtre. Paris, Gallimard, 1942. (My Theatre. Tr. Jackson Mathews. New York, Alfred A. Knopf, 1951. Contains Philoctetes [1899]; King Candaules [1901]; Saul [1903]; Bathsheba [1912]; Persephone [1934]; and the essay "The Evolution of the Theatre" [1904].)

Thésée. Paris, Gallimard, 1946. (Theseus, in Two Legends: Oedipus and Theseus. Tr. John Russell. New York, Alfred A. Knopf, 1950.)

Ainsi soit-il ou les jeux sont faits. Paris, Gallimard, 1952 (So Be It; or, The Chips Are Down. Tr. Justin O'Brien. New York, Alfred A. Knopf, 1959.)

Selections of literary criticism in Pretexts: Reflections on Literature and Morality. Ed. Justin O'Brien. Tr. Angelo P. Bertocci and others. New York, Meridian Books, 1959.

CRITICAL WORKS AND COMMENTARY

Brée, Germaine. Gide. New Brunswick, N.J., Rutgers University Press, 1963.

Delay, Jean. The Youth of André Gide. Tr. June Guicharnaud. Chicago, University of Chicago Press, 1963.

Fayer, H. M. Gide, Freedom and Dostoievsky. Burlington, Vt., Lane Press, 1946.

Hytier, Jean. André Gide. Tr. Richard Howard. Garden City, N.Y., Doubleday, 1962.

Ireland, G. W. André Gide. New York, Grove Press, 1963.

O'Brien, Justin. Portrait of André Gide: A Critical Biography. New York, Alfred A. Knopf, 1953.

Rossi, Vinio. André Gide: The Evolution of an Aesthetic. New Brunswick, N.J., Rutgers University Press, 1967.

Yale French Studies, No. 7 (1950). Special issue devoted to Gide.